Silent No More

Silent No More

Bible Women Speak Up, A Poetic Meditation

Christine Kohler

FOREWORD BY
Dandi Daley Mackall

RESOURCE *Publications* · Eugene, Oregon

Resource Publications
An Imprint of Wipf and Stock Publishers
199 W. 8th Ave., Suite 3
Eugene, OR 97401

www.wipfandstock.com

PAPERBACK ISBN: 979-8-3852-3657-2
HARDCOVER ISBN: 979-8-3852-3658-9
EBOOK ISBN: 979-8-3852-3659-6

VERSION NUMBER 11/25/24

Silent No More is dedicated to the women who have had a positive influence in my life: Nanny Franz; my stepmom, Darlene Locke, who has had the longest and most profound imprint on my life; Norma Atkins, my writing mentor; Jean Kent, who mentored me in practical life for a season; Elinore Donaldson, my spiritual mentor. These poems are dedicated to all Titus 2 women.

"I tell you, if they keep quiet, the stones will cry out."

Luke 19:40 (NIV)

Contents

Foreword by Dandi Daley Mackall

In *Silent No More: Bible Women Speak Up*, Christine Kohler draws on her skills as an experienced and studied poet, a writer of fiction and nonfiction, and a lifetime student (and teacher) of biblical studies. The result is a well-researched, deeply moving and inspiring book of timeless poetry.

I readily admit I can't identify the multiple forms of poetry employed in these pages, but I can feel the rhythm and heartbeat of each verse, the emotion of the words on every page. I've read and studied the Bible most of my adult life, but I'd never given much thought to, for instance, the Daughter of Pharoah, who pulled a babe from the water and raised Moses to manhood. Christine has made this real, live Egyptian woman unforgettable.

The same goes for the poor wife of Noah among all those animals on the Ark; or Claudia Procula before and after she warned her husband, Pilate, not to harm Jesus; or the Apostle Paul's sister, mother of Paul's nephew, who risked his life reporting to officials the overheard plot to assassinate his uncle.

Other women from the Bible, women I've studied in depth, still managed to give me numerous *Ah-ha* moments, such as the first woman, Eve, after her son Cain killed her other son, Abel.

> *. . . My anguished cries rival the howling wolves*
> *I guard my son's bloody body against.*
> *My pain is greater than when I birthed Abel.*

Adam implores me, "Come away
from the cave the raven showed us for burial."

Yet, I cannot. I cannot forsake my first born.
My soul laments, "This is my fault. Sin of my sin."
I should have cut down the Tree of Knowledge.

Out of a deep faith and understanding of the human heart and the Spirit of God, Christine Kohler offers us an invitation to go deeper. Drawing us into experiencing biblical events through the eyes, ears, heart and soul of these women, Kohler stirs our emotions and makes us eager to dig into the Scriptures and see ourselves. If we allow each evocative poem to have its way with us, to cause us to reach across the centuries and connect with women not so different from us, we will be rewarded. We will be changed, and our relationship with God will never be the same.

"Now these things happened to them as an example, and they were written for our instruction, upon whom the ends of the ages have come." I Corinthians 10:11 (NASB)

"Let this be recorded for a generation to come, so that a people not yet born may praise the Lord." Psalm 102:18 (RVS)

Dandi Daley Mackall, award-winning author of over 500 books, including *Women Who Followed Jesus: 40 Devotionals on the Journey to Easter*; and *Three Wise Women: 40 Devotions Celebrating Advent with Mary, Elizabeth, and Anna.*

Acknowledgments

I believe in giving honor where honor is due. My heart is full of gratitude to WIPFandStock for selecting *Silent No More: Bible Women Speak Up* to publish. This is the perfect house for this poetry book. Kudos to Managing Editor Matthew Wimer and his team for guiding me through this process. A hearty shout-out to the women who listened to and gave helpful comments on first drafts of select poems: Christy Albin (always the cheerleader!), Doris Holik Kelly (thanks for the title!), Lisa Bell, Wanda Strange, Vicki Woodson, and Dee Dee Ward. A special thanks to my husband, Mike Kohler, a voracious reader. Even though he admits to poetry being his least favorite genre, Mike patiently listened as I read every poem out loud. In some we discussed the theology, in others, the women's motives for what they felt. At the end, Mike is a wonderful critic and copy editor. I also want to thank Dr. Jennifer Sherman—an outstanding poet and teacher—for squeezing my book into her demanding schedule and copy editing *Silent No More*. Last, but not least, I wish to honor three women who performed "The Migrants" with little notice to compliment a sermon on Ruth and Naomi at Crossing Place Assembly of God in Granbury, Texas. Hats off to Rachel Ware, Elizabeth Black Guajardo, and Rachel Murphy. Also, thanks to the Ohio Poetry Day for selecting "Mahlah's Request to Moses, the Lawgiver" for its 2024 anthology. It was the only poem I submitted anywhere before this collection and the judges at Ohio Poetry Day showed me their faith that the poems were worth publishing. May they be a blessing to all, as those who read them blessed me with their emotional reactions.

Abbreviations

Genesis	Gen
Exodus	Exod
Number	Num
Joshua	Josh
Judges	Judg
1–2 Samuel	1–2 Sam
1 Kings	1 Kgs
Esther	Esth
Proverbs	Prov
Matthew	Matt
New International Version	NIV
Revised Standard Version	RSV

Preface

This poetry collection, *Silent No More: Bible Women Speak Up,* came to me in stages over time. However, I first committed to writing a volume of persona poems from the viewpoint of women in the Bible at a Christian Women's Bloom Conference in 2023 in south Dallas. At the Bloom Conference, women sat on a stage in a spotlight and told their stories of difficulties and redemption. I imagined what would Eve, or Rahab, or Mary Magdalene say if they were handed a microphone and asked to tell their stories. I decided that day I would put the spotlight on women in the Bible and give them the stage to pour out their hearts as to how they felt in the stories we have so often read and listened to sermons about. Sermons that often gloss over the women's actions and contributions in the struggles. When I wrote this collection, I researched the backgrounds, meditated on the scriptures, and wrote about how the women might have felt emotionally about their situations. My hope, as you read these poems, is that you will hear these women's hearts, as they speak up beyond the words on the page.

Introduction

My background is that of a journalist and author, accustomed to researching topics and digging for facts. When I wrote *Silent No More: Bible Women Speak Up* I wanted to understand the geopolitical situations of the time periods in which the women lived. I researched historical backgrounds and customs and studied an atlas as to their locations, whether in the land of Moab or beside the Sea of Galilee. I wanted to understand the physical difficulties, the prejudices against different tribes, and the restrictions on women in their societies. The more I studied, the more these women became real to me. I also wanted to know their names, so I turned to the Mishnah and Midrash, Hebrew texts that explain the law in the Torah and the gaps in the stories in the Pentateuch. It was from these sources that I found names for Noah's wife, Naahah, and Job's wife, Sitis. For New Testament women, I had no such source to turn to, so I could only give titles to Jairus's wife, Rebbetzin; Peter's mother-in-law, Fishmonger; and no name for Paul's sister. I also strived to select times in the women's lives not usually covered in Sunday Schools or literature. "Eve's Lament" takes place at the cave-tomb of Abel; "Leprous Miriam's Prayer" at the time she is isolated with leprosy; and "Michal, the King's *Eghah*" with her second husband, Phalti. This last poem from Michal is an example of how I leaned on the Jewish tradition that the couple never consummated their marriage and Phalti laid a sword in the marriage bed between them.

From an academic perspective, I balanced the book with sestinas, villanelles, and haikus in both the Old and New Testament women's poems. Most are free verse. One of my decisions for the different poetic forms was to vary the voices. I even added some lighthearted, hopefully humous, pieces to spice up the variety.

My desire is for these poems to be conversation starters to get people digging deeper into the Word and to think about these women as real people, to think deeper about their untold stories as they speak up and are silent no more.

Eve's Lament

Clawing my flesh, pouring salt into my wounds,
my anguished cries rival the howling wolves
I guard my son's bloody body against.
My pain is greater than when I birthed Abel.

Adam implores me, "Come away
from the cave the raven showed us for burial."

Yet, I cannot. I cannot forsake my firstborn.
My soul laments, "This is my fault. Sin of my sin."
I should have cut down the Tree of Knowledge,
hewed the Knowing, burned the Evil,
instead of eating the pomegranate.

I rent the bear skin my strong ruddy son Cain made.
My tears soak Abel's wooly fleeced pouch.
Adam demands, "Come away! What's done is done."

"How can I come home when our son Cain is banished,
cursed, a marked man, wandering the earth as a lost sheep?"

"Do not ever speak his name again!" Then more tenderly,
"Come away. Let our son's soul reunite with God."

I toss dirt on my son's feet.
Dust to dust.
Touch ashes from three night-watches on his head.
Ashes to ashes.

Light a torch outside the cave
with shelves hewed out for Adam and me
when we face the final death.
I kiss my fingers, touch the cold stone, linger.

"Come away," my husband pleads. "Let me embrace
you against my ribs. Let us create another son.
Bone of our bones. Flesh of our flesh.
Come away."

Naamah's Indignation with Noah

O, the indignity of it all!
My husband, Noah, asks me to trust
him, trust his faith in
an invisible God.
But this is too . . . too
sacrilege!
Noah should never
test my faith
in this one request.

For all of these years,
have I not cooked his meals,
woven his clothes,
warmed his body when cold?
Have I not gathered and mixed herbs
for poultices when he ailed?
And herded our goats
while he built the ark?

(That boat! Do not get me started
on what I have done in the name of faith
as Noah built that ludicrous house
and wove tales about how water will
fall from the heavens and cover the Earth.)

This vile creature he orders me to fetch
is the cause of our misery.
The reason why man debased
himself in lawlessness and sin.

How can my husband demand
I round up and hunt down, then
pick up those belly-slithering
fanged devils with forked tongues?
I've a mind to give Noah a tongue-
lashing of my own.

O, deceivers of Eve, I will not,
emphatically will not, touch,
nor corral, nor feed
—let the beast starve!—
snakes. *shudder*

Please, my dear husband, relieve
me of this duty. Can I not
chase down spiders instead?

Abraham Pimped Out Sarai

Sarai needed a #metoo movement
to protest sex trafficking
when her husband Abraham
pimped her to foreign kings.

Brutal betrayal recorded
in the Hebrew Logos.
Abraham pimped his wife
for cattle, sheep, oxen.

Like many abused, Sarai
hardened her heart.
No cries of sisterhood
for her handmaiden Hagar.

With patriarchal pressure
to bare a son,
Sarai pimped out her servant
to be a sex slave for Abraham.

When Hagar conceived
a healthy heir, jealous Sarai
sold Hagar not to a palace,
but to the desert to die.

Rise up, oh daughters of Sarai.
Rise up, oh daughters of Hagar.
Rise up, oh daughters of God.
Rise up, and shout #metoo #nomore

Rebekah's Supplanter

(Villanelle)

What good is a birthright
—fertile land, flocks of sheep—
if you spend life in flight?

My clever boy one night
trades lentil stew to reap
his brother Esau's rights.

To inherit all in sight
takes patience 'til Israel sleeps,
if Jacob does not take flight.

I secured my son's plight.
Stew, a trick of fur, Jacob creeps
into his father's dim light.

Enraged, Esau vows to fight.
The twins' feud runs too deep
for Jacob not to live in flight.

Schemes have led us to this plight.
All I do now is weep.
What good is a birthright
if my son spends life in flight?

Leah, Matriarch of the Tribe of Israel

Do they think I don't know they are sending Benjamin
into the jaws of Egypt? Into the lair of Pharaoh.
My son Rueben's voice shouts through the camp
like a fearful wind against the tents.
There should be no discussion.
Losing Benjamin will kill my husband.
It will kill me, too.

Yes, Benjamin is my sister Rachel's offspring.
Midwives still whisper of her death in childbirth.
For me, the memory is bittersweet as belladonna.
When Rachel travailed, crimson blood flowed from her.
Tormented screams made me rush into the tent and squat.
Drawing my sister's head against my womb, I spread my legs
around hers. Why not? We are one flesh, one blood, one tribe.

I cared for my sister as a child, taught her to draw
the water that drew Jacob to her. To us.
I did not blame Jacob for loving Rachel more.
My eye wanders toward my camel-humped nose.
Rachel possessed the grace of a gazelle dancing in the sunrise.

As life ebbed from our Rachel, a head crowned, an innocent emerged.
A wolf, a warrior, a saint. I heard it all in the child's cry.
(My husband would later name him Benjamin—
my right hand, son of my last days.)
My right arm cradled Rachel as her soul departed. My left arm held fast
to the new life, rooting on my chest for a teat long dried up.
I rubbed the blueness from his skin.

The day we laid my sister—our Rachel—in the cave,
Jacob, too, was buried.
He resurrected as Israel.
Gone was the supplanter.
God perseveres took his place.

I lifted my head, straightened my spine,
became the matriarch of the tribe of Israel.
My matron heart swelled,
proud of twelve sons and many daughters.
Joseph and Benjamin as much mine as the fruit of my womb.

Rueben's voice rises higher, floating above the tents.
He swears on the lives of his sons he will bring Benjamin home.
I drop to my knees in anguish. Bow my head to the ground.
How can he promise? Is he more omnipotent than Adonai?
We cannot endure another lost son.

Princess Bithiah, Daughter of Pharaoh, Purifies the Stench of Death

Covering my ears does not silence
the cries of drowning babies.

Shutting my eyes does not blind
me to visions of dead infants.

How can my father,
the great Egyptian Pharaoh Thutmose,
brutally slay the innocents?

I go to the Nile to wash
away the stench
of my father's sin.

I go to the Nile to purify
my soul within.

Ah, what is this amongst the reeds?
A Hebrew's basket burrowed in the bulrush.

What do I hear, but the laughter of a child?
What do I see, but the delight of a little boy?

A Hebrew baby hidden by a clever girl.
I call to her, "Bring a nursemaid."
I am not tricked by their guile.

A Hebrew, yes, I know this child is from slaves.
But I shall set him free; I shall call him son.
He shall be a prince in the palace of Pharaoh.

This Moses, drawn from the waters of Nile,
will be the redemption against my father's offence.
He shall be my revenge against his malfeasance.

Zipporah's Outcry

(Haiku)

"My bloody husband!"
I'll never forgive, forget
cutting this foreskin.

Leprous Miriam's Prayer

O Elohim, has not your servant's hands—
these now leprous hands—
protected my brother Moses
from crocs in the Nile?

O Adonai, has not these faithful feet—
my unclean feet—
rushed to fetch our mother
to nurse your Chosen One?

O Ehyey, has not these jubilant hands and feet
danced before you, Asher Ehyey?
This voice sang praises to your name.
My soul prophesied of your great mercy!

I quaked as your cloud descended.
Forgive me for slandering my sister-in-law.
My words shall be as honey sweetening mana.
I shall relinquish my brother to her care.

O Jehovah Rapha, I fall on my face before you.
Have mercy on your wretched daughter.
Heal me, Jehovah Rapha, of this disease.
Blessed be your holy name above all.

Mahlah's Request to Moses, the Lawgiver

I, Mahlah, wipe my sweaty hand on my dress,
swallow Sinai sand down my dry throat,
and gather courage to speak before Moses.
As the daughter of Zelophehad, I will say,
    "The law is unfair."
(O, Jehovah Rapha, my restorer, still my quaking.)
    "Unfair to orphaned daughters
    without male heirs to claim
    the Promised Land."

Did we not also wander in the desert?
Eating manna, washing sand from clothes and hair?
Why should we sisters not inherit our fair share?
(I must not stomp my foot when I stand before the judge.)
Did Jehovah Jireh not see fit to gift our father only daughters?
Was it not the Master of the Universe who called home
our mother and father before we reached the land of plenty?

I shall reason with the lawgiver.
When we reach the Promised Land, my sisters and I shall
    herd sheep,
    stomp grapes,
    uphold our father's righteous name
that it be not blotted out of the Torah,
which Moses records for all eternity!

Daughters should equally inherit.
This is what I will tell Moses.
Equal rights for women
    is just,
    is fair.
Equal rights should be the law.

Rahab Binds the Scarlet Cord

Quickly, my sisters, weave a scarlet cord!
The Israelites will take the city soon.
Use precious cinnabar vermilion,
a red so bright it will not be ignored.
Braid the threads tight, strong.
If our king prevail against me,
Hebrew spies shall withstand him.
A three-strand cord is not easily broken.

Hurry, father, bring mother and kindred
into the safety of my house of ill-repute.
This house which shamed you, yet fed us all,
shall be our salvation from decimation.
Do not hesitate, for Israelites are coming.
They shall vanquish Jerico—they and their God.
The God who freed them from the Egyptians.
Who parted the Red Sea. And gave them rich lands.

Let us lean out this window in the wall.
Do you see the Israeli army?
Do you hear men marching to the city gates?
Be a watchman, unafraid, as we wait
for our saviors to rescue us from the cords
of affliction, by the binding promise
of deliverance through these crimson threads.

In faith, I lower our red cord through my window.
May the God of righteousness have pity on us
who are unworthy of redemption. Yet, through a
promise sees fit to cut asunder cords of the wicked
and rescue us from bondage. In this God, do I place
my hope and our salvation.
Peering out the window, I wait.

Look, my sisters! Do you see them?
Priests, bearing the Ark of the Covenant,
circle the walls of Jerico!
Look! Behind them march an army.
Listen, for our salvation draws near.

Gather your belongings, my family.
Put on your headdresses of coins, my sisters.
For we shall adopt new kinsman.
We shall bear their sons.
So our names will not be blotted out
with the destruction of Jerico.

We shall enlarge their tents.
We shall strengthen their cords.
As their God becomes our God.
Their kingdom wealthier for it.

In expectation, we watch.
Listen.
Wait.
Trusting in a promise
as strong as the scarlet cord
hanging from my window.

Deborah's Song

Praise ye the Lord, just as he has taught me
to judge the people of Israel,
the Lord God has judged the kings of Canaan righteously.
The Lord God drowned their mighty chariots in the River Kishon,
that ancient river Kishon.

Blessed be the princes of Issachar, who followed Deborah,
as warrior woman, amongst the faint-hearted men. She rose up
as a mother leading her children into battle, guided by the Great I Am.

God told me to wake up. Wake up and speak!
Speak the words of prophecy he gave me.

From my mouth come curses and blessings.
Curse those who would not fight against the mighty.

Speak blessings to Jael, wife of Heber the Kenite, for she has dared
cut off the head of the serpent. The serpent Sisera slithered away
from battle while his soldiers turned the desert sands red with blood.

The cowardly serpent slithered into Jael's tent, asking for water. She
gave him milk and pillow to lay his head. Jael, a woman of fortitude,
hammered a tent stake through the serpent's head.
Blessed be this Kenite woman who did what no man dared.

Awake, O Deborah, my Lord tells me.
Awake, O prophetess after the likeness of Miriam, and sing.
Sing of the mercies and goodness of God's judgement.
Sing of how he has vanquished our enslavers.

Rise up, O daughters of Israel! Rise up and rejoice in the strength and victories the Lord God Almighty has wrought into our hands today and forever, and ever. Amen.

The Migrants

(Reader's Theater)

Here I am at the crossing place.
A Hebrew immigrant in a strange and foreign land.
No husband. No sons. No grandsons.
This Hebrew widow needs to cross
the Jordan River, a fluid border.
O kindred, Ephrathites, forgive my flight.

Here we are at my people's River Jordan.
Where I, Orpah, have stoically escorted Naomi
to the border of my homeland Moab.
Where I have honored my duty to my parents
to serve and obey my mother-in-law.

Here we are at the River Jordan.
Where I, Ruth, have followed Naomi
to the division of our homelands.
Why must there be a separation?
Are we not all descendants of Terah?

O daughters of Moab, I am grateful
for bread and escort through foreign lands,
treacherous to a daughter of Judah.
Behold, the Jordan River.
Turn back to your people.
I must cross alone.

My heart leaps! My tears swell.
I knew Naomi to be a kind mother,
yet I fear Israelites will not receive me.
I would rather weave mohair for Mother
than traverse the Jordan to a strange land.

With heavy heart and tears welling,
my body shakes with disbelief.
I do not wish to return to the mountains,
to a widowed mother who will turn me out
in shame. I promised to love and obey.

Do not weep, O daughters of Moab.
It is better for you to return home.
At my age, I cannot give you husbands.
You are both young and can marry from your tribe.
I am a poor widow who has given you all I had—
my sons. My precious sons.

My heartbeat quickens.
Can it be true?
My dead husband's mother
releases me!
I weep and kiss her cheek.

Wailing rises up from my chest.
I promised! "Do not send me away!
Your people will be my people.
Your God, my God.
Where you die, I will die."

Through blurry eyes, I see Orpah leave.
I pat Ruth's back and she cleaves to me.
What can I do? This daughter, now mine,
is determined to go where I go. Despite the risk.
We bundle our meager belongings onto our heads.
We step into the border waters and wade forward.
She steadies me on the journey. No turning back.

Hannah Weans Samuel

Samuel looks so angelic.
He bites my teat, smiles.
Not angry, still I pull away.
Alarmed he su-su-sucks air.
I relent, give my breast again.

Peninnah, my tormentor,
chides me to wean Samuel.
Secretly, I know it is time.
Still, how can I relinquish
my only child to the priest Eli?

I sent my husband Elkanah
to the annual sacrifice at temple
without me. I'm sure it pleased
his second wife, Peninnah. Yet,
I need this time preparing Samuel.

When my son is weaned,
I will fulfill my promise
to leave him with the priests
as my sacrifice in service, as
my dedication to my Lord.

Samuel is done eating, playing.
He sleeps soundly against my chest.
Vulnerable, angelic. What does
he see behind his closed eyelids?
Visions befitting a priest? A prophet?

When he is weaned,
we'll go to the temple.
On my honor,
I promised
my son.

Bathsheba Confesses Her Sins

I confess my sins, O Lord.
Punish me instead
of taking my son's life.

I confess,
I should not have heeded
adulterous lust and come
into David's bedchamber.

I confess,
I disobeyed Your law during
my purification period.
Absolution for the unclean.

I confess,
I betrayed my husband Uriah.
I should have repented to him
while he camped at palace gates.

I confess,
I should not have fretted David.
Did I drive Uriah to front lines?
His blood is on my hands.

O God, my Lord,
I confess. I beg of you,
save my innocent son.
Take my life instead.

To be queen among many
without a male heir
is to be one concubine
in a harem of thousands.

Without a son,
my life is like the sand
under my feet.
Of no value. No future.

O Lord, I confess,
my sins are legion.
Selfishness, covetousness.
Numbering more than stars.

I confess.

Weep for Michal, the Foster Mother

Weep, O women of Israel, for Michal,
a childless queen who fostered
her sister Merob's five sons.

Blessed be Michal of the house of Saul
and the favored house of David
whose heart enlarged for orphaned boys.

She wallowed not in pity from barrenness.
Instead, Michal mothered her nephews.
Blessed be foster mothers!

O women of Israel, weep for Michal.
Her husband, King David, sacrificed
Merob's five grown sons. Executed.

Gibeonites' blood-thirsty revenge.
Hanging from a tree, all five men
Michal mothered since boyhood.

Weep, O women of Israel, for Michal.

Rizpah's Grief on the Execution of her Sons

"Eli, Eli, lema sabachthani?"

My sons hang desecrated
from a bloody rood,
stained by their royal veins.

My fiery grief unquenchable
as I shake my fist at fowl
and Elohim.

David—(I shall not call him my king)—
sacrificed my sons and the sons of his wife,
Michal, whom she reared for her dear sister,
to the Gibeonites, who sought revenge.

The kingdom usurper David claimed
it was to end the three-year drought.
Yet, I know he complied to slaughter
all claims to his precious Israeli throne.

"Let their blood be on the Gibeonites," he said.
No. No! The shame is David's, who stole the crown
from my dead lover, Saul, the father of my slain sons.

I shall not leave this place of desolation
until David makes restitution to me and Michal
by burying our sons whose bodies
are defiled by blood-thirsty vultures and beasts.

I shall not leave my sons, even if I be swallowed by death.
"My God, my God, why have you forsaken me?"

Michal, the King's *Eghah*

My beloved, my David
calls me *Eghah*, his calf,
as a term of endearment.
Yet, my father, King Saul
mocks me, trading me as a cow
to another man, Phalti, to marry.

This sham marriage is a joke.
But, Phalti is no jester,
as he lays his sword
between us in our marriage bed.
Though his tears betray his longing.

And I am no fool. He fears
my beloved who paid a dowry
of two hundred Philistine foreskins
to wed me as his wife. My beloved
David would slay Phalti with his sword
if he consummates this marriage.

As I lie here, smelling his sweat
like sandalwood, so different
from David's scent of wool and woods,
I am not deceived. My father betrayed
me also out of fear—a powerful motivator.
Fear David will seize his crown through me.

O, how long will it be, my love,
until you rescue me, my king?
Are you waiting to see whom I will choose?
My father Saul, or you, my husband David?
In name, I may be Phalti's wife,
but, in truth, I am your *Eghah*.

The Zidon Widow's Faith

I stand at the bottom of my stairs and listen
for my son's voice. My dead son's voice.
Yet, I only hear loud prayers from the prophet.
Booming pleas to his one God, Yahweh.
The God who stretched my meal and oil.
A miracle, he claims. But bringing my son
back to life? For that I lack faith to believe.

I rub the amulet hid beneath my goat-hair robe.
Elijah must not know I kept the worry stone.
That first day in my home, he threw out my icons—
Ba'al Hammon, Ashtoreth, and Eshmun—
and forbade me to go to the temple to worship.
I complied because of the magic the prophet
performed that kept us fed throughout this drought.

I stand before the window, gazing at the sea.
I am not aware of how I got here in my pacing
and rubbing the stone. In waiting, my mind wanders.
How can there be so much water in the Mediterranean
Sea, yet so little rain. Is Ba'al Hammon deaf? Is Yahweh?
Elijah must not know, but I pray to them both. Why not?
Still, neither god answers. Not even when priests pray.

Now Elijah has taken my only son—my dead son—
upstairs to beg his God, Yahweh, to resurrect my precious boy.
How can a God who withholds rain and curses the ground,
a God who allowed my son to die, how can I believe he cares
and will restore the breath of life to my child? I am tempted
to flee to the temple and prostrate myself before Eshumun,
god of healing. Why should I stay and trust the God of Elijah?

The prophet's voice crescendos through my rooftop.
Enough! I rush to the stairs. I will take my son's body
to the Temple of Ba'al and beg Eshumun to either heal
my child, or carry his soul to the afterlife. No more, Elijah!
My feet take flight to the door. I fling it open. My son
sits up and asks for a meal cake. I stop, stunned. He lives!
Praise God, Yahweh. Elijah truly is a man of God. I believe!

Esther in the Harem

(Sestina)

Truly, I am not ready.
Uncle says God has purpose.
If I lean on Shaddai's source,
he promises me good gifts.
I descend from King Saul's queen.
Mordecai reared me prepared.

Yet, when taken, how prepared
could I be? I'm not ready
to replace Vashti, the queen.
I'm frightened of the purpose,
mystified by the king's gifts
given after such force.

Oil, myrrh, trained well in discourse
Seven handmaidens prepared
me. Plus, rewarded with gifts
beyond measure. Still, ready?
How could I be when the purpose
is to reign Persia as queen?

My sad heart aches for the queen
who refused, with no remorse,
King Ahasuerus, whose purpose
would degrade the queen. Prepared,
but not possibly ready
for dethronement, no grace gifts.

Unlike others, it's not gifts
I desire as a queen.
Higher stakes cause me to ready
my temple as a resource.
A bride must be prepared
for a far greater purpose.

Though I don't know God's purpose,
I yield myself to his gifts,
do my best to be prepared.
Even though becoming a queen
means I must have intercourse
with the king. I'm not ready!

My purpose: to be queen,
My gifts: Rely on God's source.
Prepared. Yet still not ready.

The Suffering of Sitis, Job's Wife

My anguish is unquenchable.
My soul, unconsolable.
My husband and his God
do nothing to ease my pain.

Does Job not see me in sackcloth
and ashes, screaming like the gulls,
weeping enough to fill the seas,
for our dead sons and daughters?

My tears soak the garment of our eldest,
a cloak I wove and sewed for him.
He was our life, our future namesake.
His death has stripped me of all hope.

My beautiful daughters, my crowning jewels,
crushed beneath the walls demolished
by a whirlwind from the wilderness.
Where was God in the sandstorm?

My husband does obeisance before him.
He calls me a fool when I curse the defense
of slaughtering our children and servants.
It is I who lack courage to curse God and die.

So, I lash out at my husband, Job, instead.
Does he take me in his arms, be understanding?
No! A thousand times no!
Yet, Job pours out his despair to his friends.

Who is here to comfort me in my darkest days?
Who is here to hold me close and not judge
the depth of my grief? Who will listen to my suffering?
No one. I am alone and shaking with rage at my loss.

A Proverbs 31 Parody

Who can find a virtuous woman?

Oy, give me a break!
My fingers are rubbed raw
from spinning threads.
Looms make my joints ache.
Needles prick while sewing
fine linen clothing,
coveted in the agora place.

Who can find a virtuous woman?

Oy vey, stop looking.
At least for one day!
Burning midnight oil,
rising before sunrise,
no time for nosh or kvetch.
Elohim, gird my loins with strength.
Heal my tongue from biting it.

Who can find a virtuous woman?
Her price is far above rubies.

As if fashion designer in haute couture,
merchant, businesswoman, cook,
is bupkis. My husband, the mensch,
says buy land, run a vineyard.

Plant, harvest, make wine.
Less kibbitz at the city gate,
my love. I beg of you!

Her children arise up, call her blessed.
Her husband praises her.

Meshugaas. Nonsense!
Rather than adulations,
pitch in and help without prompting.
Many hands make work light.
Cover me with my tapestry
for one blessed night
and let me sleep past a cock crow.

She shall rejoice in time to come.

In time? When? Don't futz with me.
After my last breath? Oy vey.
After I no longer clean, cook, weave,
sew, sell, and manage the vineyard?
Praise is better from another's lips.
Yes! Leave me verklempt—swooning!
Praise me now, not in eulogy.

L'chaim!

Bethlehem Nights

(Haiku)

Mary rocks her son
Soft winds whisper lullabies
On wings of angels

The Fishmonger's Miracle

"Peter means well."
His mother-in-law sighed, wiped her brow.
Vinegar brine permeated the room
from dirt floor to thatched roof.
The fishmonger flushed as she pickled sardines.
Was it hot that fall day? Or was it her?
Where was the breeze from Galilee Sea?
Only flies buzzed through open windows.

Her mind drifted to her son-in-law.
Dismayed when her husband brought Simon
to their daughter. He was course, rash, brash.
Impulsive. Imperious. Stubborn as a mule.
"Yet, under it all, a good heart," she murmured.
"After all, he took me in, didn't he?"
Even afterward, she stayed. "May peace be upon her."
Sadness chilled the elderly woman. She shuddered.

If only her precious daughter had lived
to see the changes in Simon, now called Peter
by the Nazarene. At first, she moaned
her son-in-law's derelict to fishing.
"We'll starve!" she'd warned
when he left the sea and followed the prophet.
She grumbled as she mended Simon's nets
and traded pickled sardines for bread.

Instead of fish, Peter talked of faith and hope,
kingdoms to come. He regaled sermons and stories
of Rabbi doing miracles. "He wants me to believe!
How can I when I'm here working? Bah!
How can I believe Jesus walks on water? Or divides
fish and loaves? Or tax money from a carp's mouth?"
She held her aching head. The room spun.
Sweat poured beneath her cloak.

Pushing the pickling aside, she needed to bake fish.
Soon guests would arrive. Especially the Nazarene,
whom Peter had confided might be the Messiah.
Dared she hope? How could she have faith? Oh, to believe!
Pouring olive oil in a pan, she fileted Tilapia. Clutching a chair,
she collapsed to the floor. Burning. So hot . . . must be fever.
Light poured in. Cool hands touched her. Hands that held a miracle.
She rose up in health—her heart full of faith—and fixed dinner.

Joanna's Eternal Gratitude

I will never understand
how those who were lepers,
deaf, mute, lame—once delivered—
do not bother to thank the Healer.
Where is their attitude of gratitude?

I confess my sin of occult.
I left Yahweh of my youth,
pursued false gods at Roman temples.
In thanks, demons and disease
took over my body, stole my control.

It almost ruined my marriage with Chuzza.
It affected my husband's job with Herod.
My unspeakable behavior did cost me
my dignity, my sanity, my health.
Oh, how humiliation dogged me.

Then I met a man—no, not just any man—
a Rabbi, a Healer, One with the power
to command demons to leave, disease to go.
This man Jesus, surely the Messiah,
I bow to in eternal gratitude and service.

The Rebbetzin Laments her Daughter

My husband asks me to trust him,
but how can I? Our only daughter
is feverish and near death.
Yet, how can I not trust him?
Otherwise is to admit defeat,
accept the worst as inevitable.

Jairus, a chief Rabbi at the synagogue,
says he knows a remarkable Rabbi,
Jesus, who heals better than a physician.
My husband has left to find this miracle
wonder-worker. Meanwhile, I wipe her brow
and pray fervently. What delays them?

My heart aches as mourners wail
outside her bedroom door, as if she
were already dead. I cover my ears
and weep for my sweet daughter.
So bright, as I teach her Hebrew while
we embroider. At 12, she can cook, too.

My precious daughter, almost of age,
goes still, fluids release, lips blue, skin cold.
An animal scream emits from me.
I do not notice the door opening until
my husband's arms pull me away from
our daughter, who is clearly dead.

Beside him stands three men. One must be
the Great Physician. Why did he tarry?
I want left alone. Yet the Master speaks
with authority. Jesus insists our daughter
is not dead. Either crazy or a true man of God.

Jairus holds me as wailing and laughter drifts
through the bedroom wall. Such disrespect
when I should be preparing her for burial.
"Rise, my child!" the Healer says, as if she naps.
Her eyes blink. Pink color tinges her skin.
Our daughter lives! Surely, he is the Messiah!

Martha, Four Days

Four days.
My brother, Lasarus, dead
four days.
Day one, my sister, Mary, and I covered him in burial spices.
Day one, we wrapped our brother's body in grave cloths.
Day one, friends carried Lasarus, gone too young, into a cave.
Night one, strong men rolled a stone before the opening,
blocking out all light. Killing all hope.

Four days.
Mary wept.
What will happen to us?
No father. No brother. No husbands.
How will we support ourselves?
Society can be cruel to single women.
Before Lasarus died
I sent word of my brother's illness to Jesus.
Then waited. Waited. And waited.

Four days.
Like water heating over fire,
anxiousness roiled into anger,
boiling for four days.
Does my Lord not love us?
How could he have stayed away
until my brother's corpse rotted
four days.

High Priests threatened to stone Jesus.
The Messiah—the Son of God!—
transcends fear, stoning, and death.
If Jesus had only come,
Lazarus would not have died.
I would stake my life on it.
Now the Healer was four days
too late. Too late for a miracle.

Martha, Be Not Troubled

No matter how much I smile
while serving lamb stew
I cannot shake from memory
the voice of Jesus chiding me,
"Martha, be not troubled."

How could I not worry?
Orphaned, I carry the first-born
burdens. Pretty Mary is so flighty.
Lazarus, my precious brother, died!
How does one not be anxious?

Lazarus is our protector against ruin,
our financial support against poverty.
Chills run through me, thinking how
lost my sister and I were at his tomb.
How scared I felt when Jesus delayed.

Setting the steaming stew before my Lord,
I ladle it carefully into the men's bowls,
giving extra spoonfuls to Jesus and Lazarus.
My heart bursts with gratitude,
leaving no room for panic or fretting.

Mary Prepares for Passover

Six days before Passover,
Jesus is coming to dinner.
John the Baptist once called
him, "The Lamb of God."
Yet, I call him my friend.
Still, I think on what it means.

All the miracles, especially for us.
Raising my brother from the dead!
Oh, how deeply Jesus loves us.
What can I do to ever repay him?
I did not complain when helping
Martha fix the meal. Did he notice?

I cannot leave my place to serve.
I hunger for the Master's word.
I fear this will be our last supper.
People threaten to stone him.
Lambs are sacrificed, like the Baptist.
It's six days before Passover.

Rising from the table,
I fetch spikenard oil.
Baptize the feet of Jesus.
I dry the drenched Lamb,
and my tears, with my hair,
Six days before Passover.

Salome's Request for her Sons

They are hard workers,
my sons James and John.
And they work hard for Jesus.
Was my request unreasonable?
No, said I.

At first, we knew him as Rabboni.
A good way to advance
from fisherman to scholar,
I told my husband Zebedee.
He agreed.

Then the Rabbi healed.
A physician, even better skill
for my bright and gifted boys.
"Learn!" I urged James and John.
They obeyed.

"The kingdom of God is near,"
the Rabbi-Physician, Jesus, preached.
Ah, so he plans to overthrow Rome.
My sons are following a king!
Come, I said.

"Master, grant this one request.
As your good and faithful disciples,
may my sons rule by your royal side
when you establish your kingdom.
I bowed.

"You don't know what you ask.
Can they drink of my cup?
Can they be baptized by fire?"
Such riddles this future king speaks.
"They can," said we.

"You can drink of my cup,
be immersed with my baptism.
But the places of position
are decided by my Father."
I heard hope.

Salome's Revelation

How could I have been so wrong
about the Kingdom of Christ?

I am still reeling
with shock,
grief,
fear.

My God! My God!
Did you truly forsake
your only begotten son?
My Lord Jesus is dead.

At his last breath,
the sky blackened,
the earth trembled,
and my heart broke.

I am shaken
with shock,
grief,
fear.

A priest screamed,
bells tinkling wildly
as he ran. The Holy of Holies
exposed. The veil ripped in half.

I rubbed my eyes, not believing
my great-uncle, dead three weeks,
walked the streets—alive and well!
I called his name. He waved.

I know not what is true
or false.
Spirit,
or flesh.

The kingdom of which Jesus spoke,
could he be a heavenly ruler instead?

Then what did I ask of the prophet?
What cup and baptism will my sons endure?

I am confused
with shock,
grief,
fear.

God, help my sons, John and James.
Though the sky blackens,
the earth trembles,
and my heart breaks.

Claudia Procula Warns her Husband Pilatus

I must warn him. It is a trap
these unholy priests have set
for my husband Pontius Pilatus.

Pilatus is a wise prefect of Judea,
but he does not know the facts
of this case brought before him.

Last night on my bed I suffered
night terrors, dreaming of Christ
the Messiah falsely accused.

I swear the Hebrew God himself
visited in my sleep so I would warn
Pilatus not to condemn God's Son.

Least I be mistaken, I called servants
who told disturbing reports of betrayal,
blood money, and suicide by hanging.

Fearfully, I wrote a note warning
my beloved, "Jesus the Messiah
is innocent. God told me in dreams."

I hide behind the Seat of Judgement.
My husband offers Barabbas instead.
"Crucify Christ!" the crowd yells.

My husband washes his hands of guilt.
He knows I would not interfere lightly.
"I am innocent of this man's blood."

Clutching my heart, relief still does not come.
Though Pilatus absconded responsibility.
The blood-thirsty mob cries, "Crucify Christ!"

Three Marys at the Tomb

(A Reader's Theater)

(Chorus)
Let us get spices for Jesus' body.
This one thing we can do
for his mother, Mary.

If I, Mary Salome, were literate,
I would write my sister's story.
I was there, holding her hand,
yet confused, when she confided
of her mysterious pregnancy.

If I, Mary Cleophus, were gifted in drama,
I would recount untold tales of adventure
my sister-in-law told of Magi and Egypt.
Home again to Nazareth, we reared our boys
together. I believed Mary, believed in Jesus.

If I, Mary Magdalene, were an alchemist
I would have bottled the many tears
of my Lord's mother, my friend.
Misunderstood, harassed, then crucified.
No mother should bear such torment.

(Chorus)
Let us get spices for Jesus' body.
This one thing we can do
for his mother, Mary.

Let us gather frankincense and myrrh.
May the sweet fragrance remind Mary
of her son's birth in a Bethlehem stable.
May the fragrance be pleasing to God.

(Chorus)
Let us get spices for Jesus' body.
This one thing we can do
for his mother, Mary.
For our sister and friend, for Mary.

Sapphira's Lie

(Villanelle)

My husband demands I lie.
He takes from me the land deed.
I am afraid I will die.

A piece of land he did buy
and sell. The church has a need.
My husband demands I lie.

Ananias says, "Don't pry!"
But I knew his depth of greed.
I am afraid I will die.

I only want to know, "Why?"
He insists I take his lead.
My husband demands I lie.

I beg to speak truth, then sigh.
He turns stone deaf when I plead.
I am afraid I will die.

The apostles come nigh.
They ask for the lucre seed.
My husband demands I lie.
I am afraid I will—

Coverings of Love

Weep not, O Widows.
You who clutch tight
the garments sewn
in love and compassion
by blood-pricked fingers.

Quick, fetch the fisherman, they cry.
The one who walked with the Healer.
The Master who rose from the dead.
Surely his disciple can awaken Tabitha.
Awaken her from eternal sleep.

Weep not, O Widows.
You who are covered
with blankets of grace
woven by calloused hands
of the almsgiver Tabitha.

Fisherman Peter, disciple of Christ
the Healer, runs swiftly to Joppa.
His heart beats for the widows
whose anguish cries in need
of the Messiah's healing touch.

Weep not, O Widows.
Make way for the one
who followed Jesus
who cares for the widows
who blesses the seamstress.

Arise, Tabitha, arise!
Death cannot hold a saint
so covered in love
by those she comforted
through prayer cloths.

Rejoice, O Widows!
For resurrection power
by the blood of the Lamb
whose woolen fleece was woven
for your covering. Your Comforter.

Rejoice! She lives!

Paul's Sister Prays

What danger has my brother Paul gotten my son into?

My boy was called to the palace to give testimony
against the high priests. I don't trust them not to retaliate.
Even though our father was a Pharisee, a noble man.

Look at what they turned my brother into, a hunter
of innocent men. My heart still breaks for Stephen's
mother. I know the disciple's death haunts my brother.

Ever since Paul's blinding epiphany and conversion
to Christ, he has been a role model for his nephew, my son.
But I never expected Paul to appear in Jerusalem in chains.

My son could not stay away. He insisted on seeing his uncle.
He heard Paul preach in Hebrew of Christ, saw the priests
riled into a frenzy, hatching a plot to kill my brother, Paul.

My son is noble man, like my father. He could not stand by
and allow Paul to be assassinated. My son is a brave boy.
Yet, I worry the priests will turn their anger on him, do harm.

In anguish, I am afraid for my son. So, I pray, not as my father,
a Pharisee, a priest, directed me to pray. Instead, I pray, as Paul,
my brother, taught me. In the name of Jesus Christ, my Lord.

I commend my son into your hands, to do your will, my God and Savior.

Amen.

www.ingramcontent.com/pod-product-compliance
Lightning Source LLC
Chambersburg PA
CBHW072023060426
42449CB00034B/2073